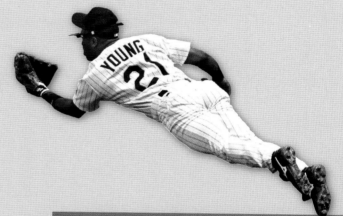

THE STORY OF THE
**COLORADO ROCKIES**

GRANDSTAND SEAT $ 6.00
Est. Price $5.00 · Tax $1.00 · **TOTAL**

Right hereby reserved to refund said price
and revoke license granted by this ticket.

SEC.
**14**
ROW
**8**
SEAT
**10**
GAME
**4**

**DAY GAME**
THE BALLPARK
★    ★
American League
vs.
National League

Read Important
Notices on
Reverse Side
★
Do Not Detach
This Coupon From
Rain Check

GAME
**4**

**RAIN CHECK**
SEC.
**14**

**DAY GAME**
GRANDSTAND SEAT $ 6.00
Est. Price $5.00
Fed. Tax $1.00 · **TOTAL**

Right hereby reserved to refund said price and revoke
license granted by this ticket.

READ IMPORTANT NOTICES
ON REVERSE SIDE

ROW
**8**
SEAT
**10**
GAME
**4**

Published by Creative Education
P.O. Box 227, Mankato, Minnesota 56002
Creative Education is an imprint of The Creative Company

Design and production by Blue Design
Printed in the United States of America

Photographs by Corbis (Jan Butchofsky-Houser), Getty Images (Brian Bahr, Al Bello/Allsport, Nathan Bilow/Allsport, TIMOTHY A. CLARY/AFP, DOUG COLLIER/AFP, Tim de Frisco/Allsport, Stephen Dunn/Allsport, David L. Greene/MLB Photos, Jeff Gross, Jed Jacobsohn, Rob Leiter/MLB Photos, Ronald Martinez, Donald Miralle, Bernie Nunez/Allsport, Doug Pensinger, Jamie Squire, Todd Warshaw/Allsport, CHRIS WILKINS/AFP, Michael Zagaris/MLB Photos)

Library of Congress Cataloging-in-Publication Data

Omoth, Tyler.
The story of the Colorado Rockies / by Tyler Omoth.
p. cm. — (Baseball: the great American game)
Includes index.
ISBN-13: 978-1-58341-486-6
1. Colorado Rockies (Baseball team)—History—Juvenile literature. I. Title. II. Series.

GV875.C78O56 2007
796.357'640978883—dc22          2006034142

First Edition
9 8 7 6 5 4 3 2 1

Cover: First baseman Todd Helton
Page 1: Second baseman Eric Young
Page 3: Outfielder Matt Holliday

THE STORY OF THE
# COLORADO
# ROCKIES

by Tyler Omoth

JASON JENNINGS

# Colorado Rockies

t's the top of the ninth inning of a 9–0 blowout at New York's Shea Stadium on August 23, 2001. On the mound, New York Mets reliever Donne Wall stares down rookie pitcher Jason Jennings of the Colorado Rockies. Although neither team would see the playoffs this year, this at bat would be the exclamation point at the end of a masterful major-league debut for Jennings: after pitching eight

innings of shutout ball, hitting two singles, and driving in a run, Jennings takes a powerful stroke at Wall's offering and sends it over the left-field fence. As Jennings crosses the plate, he becomes the first baseball player ever to pitch a complete-game shutout and hit a home run in his first major-league game. On an August day in the

midst of a disappointing 73–89 season, weary Colorado fans see a glimmer of hope in Jennings and their beloved Rockies.

# MILE-HIGH EXPECTATIONS

**D**enver, the capital of Colorado, is known as "The Mile-High City" because of its extreme elevation. Situated on the plains just east of the Rocky Mountains, Denver's location has made it a vital hub in the transportation and distribution of goods in the mountain states of America. Denver is also recognized as a great sports city. It is home to the National Football League's Denver Broncos, the National Basketball Association's Denver Nuggets, and the National Hockey League's Colorado Avalanche. Until almost two decades ago, baseball had never had a professional presence in Colorado.

In 1985, Major League Baseball permitted the National League (NL) to expand by two teams. With a number of cities competing for the proposed franchises, Colorado went above and beyond its competitors' efforts by initiating a search for an ownership group, making plans to build a stadium, and even beginning to sell season tickets. It wasn't until 1991, though, that the decision became official: the two new teams would be awarded to Denver and Miami, Florida. The Colorado Baseball Partnership, led by banking executive Larry Varnell, announced that the team would be called the Colorado Rockies, and the group unveiled a purple-mountain design that would be the team's logo.

Once the Rockies had been established as an expansion franchise, the

**ANDRES GALARRAGA** – Before becoming the first star player to join the Rockies, Galarraga was a brilliant fielder and feared slugger with the Montreal Expos. In 1997, he crushed an upper-deck home run at Miami's Pro Player Stadium that was measured at 573 feet.

# A WARM WELCOME FOR BASEBALL

The questions that major-league officials must consider each time a league expansion is proposed are many. But no factor weighs as heavily for a city that is in the running for a team than that of attendance: Can they fill the seats? The Colorado Rockies' fans answered that question with a resounding "yes" during the club's inaugural season in 1993 by becoming the fastest team ever to reach the one-million mark in attendance (by Mother's Day, May 9). As if that wasn't impressive enough, the Rockies also set the mark for fastest to two million fans (June 20) and three million (July 28). By September 17 of the first season the big leagues were in Colorado, four million fans had attended Rockies games at Mile High Stadium, breaking the all-time mark for a baseball expansion team. The final tally at season's end was a whopping 4,483,350. The team continued to be number one in yearly attendance in the NL through the 1999 season. Even though the club's success on the field has been limited, the people of Colorado have proven time and again that they love their baseball.

next step was to build a front office and roster. Bob Gebhard was named general manager in September 1991. In October 1992, Colorado appointed former major-league player and hitting coach Don Baylor as manager. Although Baylor lacked experience as a manager at the professional level, the move would prove to be a good one. "I didn't know if he could manage," acknowledged Gebhard, "but I thought if there ever was an opportunity for someone to step into a manager's role and learn, it would be with an expansion ballclub. So I took a chance with Don."

Soon after Baylor was hired, an expansion draft was held that allowed Colorado and the new Florida Marlins to select unprotected players from other major-league teams. The Rockies added to their pitching staff with the first pick, taking David Nied from the Atlanta Braves. The team also signed five-time All-Star first baseman Andres "The Big Cat" Galarraga as a free agent, adding a legitimate slugger to its lineup.

ERIC YOUNG

**ERIC YOUNG** – Young provided abundant speed and solid fielding during the Rockies' first five seasons. In 1995, the second baseman led the NL in triples (9). He followed that up by stealing a league-leading 53 bases in 1996, a feat that earned him a place on the NL All-Star team.

## PITCHER · PEDRO ASTACIO

A ground-ball pitcher who was undaunted by the thin air of Colorado, Pedro Astacio set Rockies club records for innings pitched, complete games, and career victories. He didn't always rely on just ground balls, though; he also became the most prolific strikeout pitcher in Rockies history. Astacio's durability earned him the nickname "Mula" from his teammates, which is Spanish for "mule." The Dominican-born pitcher was a fiery competitor who wore his emotions on his sleeve, making him entertaining to watch every time he took the mound. After his years with the Rockies, Astacio's endurance began to fade, though, and he moved around the major and minor leagues as a member of several other teams.

PEDRO ASTACIO
PITCHER

COLORADO
ROCKIES

### STATS

**Rockies seasons: 1997–2001**

**Height: 6-2**

**Weight: 210**

- **1,664 career strikeouts**

- **31 career complete games**

- **12 career shutouts**

- **129–124 career record**

## CATCHER · JEFF REED

Jeff Reed discovered firsthand what Colorado's clean, cool, thin mountain air could do to revitalize a baseball player's career. Reed, who played for six teams and personified the role of journeyman catcher, saw his statistics improve dramatically in his years with the Rockies. A career .250 hitter, he batted .286 during his three-and-a-half-year stay in Colorado. In 1997, he sent 17 home runs over the fence—the only time he ever broke 10 homers in a season. Known as a solid defensive backstop, Reed helped Rockies pitchers put together three of the franchise's best overall seasons in 1996, 1997, and 1998.

### STATS

**Rockies seasons: 1996–99**

**Height: 6-2**

**Weight: 190**

- **.988 career fielding percentage**
- **.250 career BA**
- **.334 career on-base percentage**
- **1,234 career games**

**JEFF REED**
CATCHER

COLORADO
ROCKIES

After years of hoping and waiting, Colorado baseball fans watched their Rockies play their first game on April 5, 1993, with Nied on the mound. Although the game was a 3–0 loss in New York to the Mets, it marked the beginning of a new era for baseball and for Colorado sports fans. While Nied was the pitcher of record for the Rockies' first loss, he would also throw the franchise's first strikeout, first walk, first complete game, and first complete-game shutout that season.

Since the new Coors Field was not yet finished, the Rockies played their first-season home games in Mile High Stadium, home of the Denver Broncos football team. At their home opener against the Montreal Expos on April 9, the Rockies gave fans a taste of baseball Colorado-style as second baseman Eric Young led off the bottom of the first inning by slamming a home run and bringing the major-league-record crowd of 80,227 fans to its feet. The team went on to win the game 11–4, but by the end of the season, it found itself in last place in the NL Western Division.

# A MOUNTAIN OF A SEASON

ot surprisingly, the first two seasons of Rockies baseball were not very successful. After finishing 67–95 in 1993, the team came in third in the strike-shortened 1994 season, going 53–64. Even though baseball fans across the country were discouraged by the 1994 players' strike, the Rockies faithful were not deterred and continued to pass through the turnstiles, setting several major-league attendance records. The Rockies drew their three-millionth fan in only the 52nd home game of the 1994 season, beating their record from 1993 by one day.

The team made a splash in the 1995 free-agent market by signing Larry Walker, a solid-hitting right fielder from the Montreal Expos, just one week after the strike ended in April 1995. On April 26, the Rockies played their first game in the newly completed Coors Field. The 14-inning battle with the Mets ended when Colorado left fielder Dante Bichette launched a game-winning, three-run home run in the bottom of the 14th inning, giving the Rockies an 11–9 victory. By the end of April, the Rockies had a 4–1 record and led the NL West. Fans had a feeling that this year would be different.

Colorado's four big-time bashers put together an impressive 1995 season,

Larry Walker was a rarity, a brawny slugger who won numerous Gold Glove awards for his defense.

LARRY WALKER

## FIRST BASEMAN · TODD HELTON

Perhaps no player was as valuable to the Rockies as Todd Helton. A three-time Gold Glove winner, he held the highest career statistics of any Rockies player for batting average (.333), hits (1,700), doubles (413), home runs (286), and RBI (996) through 2006. After being called up to the majors in 1997, Helton quietly earned a place among the NL's elite hitters with his combination of solid contact hitting and impressive power. A clubhouse leader and fan favorite, he spent his entire major-league career in Rockies purple.

**TODD HELTON**
FIRST BASEMAN

COLORADO ROCKIES

### STATS

**Rockies seasons: 1997–present**

**Height: 6-2**

**Weight: 210**

- **2000 NL leader in BA (.372)**

- **286 career HR**

- **5-time All-Star**

- **413 career doubles**

during which the Rockies became only the second team in major-league history to have 4 teammates hit 30 or more home runs in a single season (after the Los Angeles Dodgers accomplished the feat in 1977). All season long, Bichette, Galarraga, Walker, and third baseman Vinny Castilla wreaked havoc on opposing pitchers. A local newspaper columnist dubbed the foursome the "Blake Street Bombers" for their "long bomb" exploits at Coors Field, located on Blake Street in Denver. Together, these players powered the Rockies' offense with more than 400 runs batted in (RBI) and slugged more than 130 home runs during the Rockies' pennant-chasing season—a feat put into perspective by the fact that 11 other big-league teams failed to produce that many home runs using the entire lineup.

Part of the Bombers' success could be attributed to their home field, which naturally favored hitters over pitchers. The mile-high altitude of Denver's Coors Field, with its reduced air pressure, meant that baseballs thrown at the park had a greater chance of being hit, since there was less movement on breaking pitches. And once a bat smacked a ball, there was less resistance on the ball's flight, causing it to travel farther at Coors than at "normal" ballparks with lower elevations.

But hot bats and thin air were not the only things that helped the 1995 Rockies achieve a second-place, 77–67 finish; steady veteran leadership was also key. Shortstop Walt Weiss hit only one home run for the team that year,

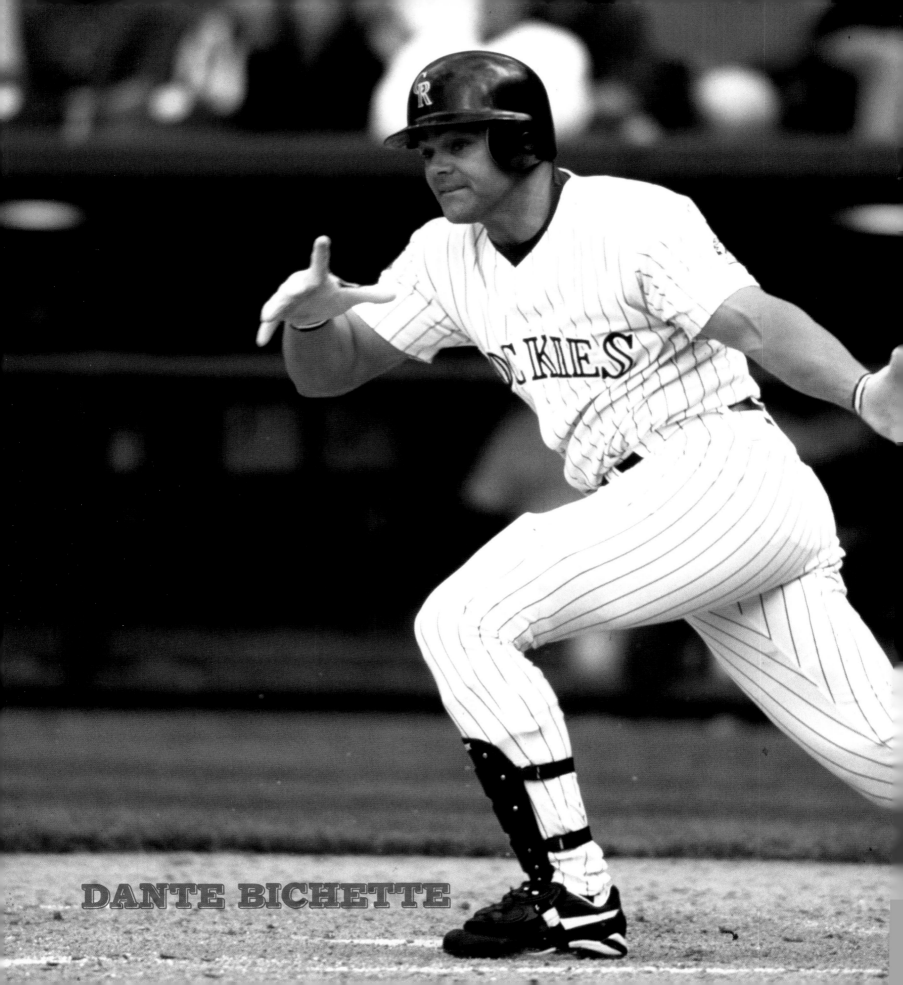

DANTE BICHETTE

## 30-30 VISION

During the 1996 season, the Rockies reached their all-time high in victories with 83, an achievement they matched the next year. But on September 13, 1996, the Rockies found their way into the record books in rare fashion. The previous day, outfielder Ellis Burks had punched his card into an elite club, having achieved 30 steals and 30 home runs in one season. He knocked his 30th home run out of the park in early August, and on September 12, he managed to swipe his 30th base of the season, becoming one of only a handful of major-leaguers to reach that milestone. The real rarity came the next night during a home game versus the Houston Astros, when left fielder Dante Bichette (who had stolen his 30th base the night before) sent his 30th home run over the left-field wall to become the second member of the 1996 Colorado Rockies to join the 30-30 club. The only other time that two members of the same team had accomplished the feat occurred when the New York Mets' Howard Johnson and Darryl Strawberry combined for 68 stolen bases and 75 home runs in 1987.

but his leadership and solid defensive play kept the team focused when it was out on the field. His double-play partner, second baseman Eric Young, sparked the team on the base paths by stealing 35 bases. The pitching staff was led by Kevin Ritz, who ended the season 11–11 but started 28 games for the Rockies, eating up 173.3 innings—nearly 70 innings more than any other pitcher on Colorado's staff.

An August slump tested the team's resolve, but Colorado rallied to win 14 of its last 20 regular-season games. The Rockies' postseason hopes rested on the last game of the season. If they won, they would earn a Wild Card berth, even though they were in second place in the NL West. If they lost, they would have to face the Houston Astros (who owned an identical record) in a special one-game playoff. Thanks largely to runs by Young, Walker, and catcher Joe Girardi, the Rockies pulled off a 10–9 comeback victory over the San Francisco Giants on October 1 to capture the Wild Card and advance to meet the Atlanta Braves in the NL Division Series (NLDS).

Colorado's first venture into the postseason was short-lived, as the heavily favored Braves topped the Rockies three games to one, despite fine performances by Castilla, Young, and Bichette. Baylor tipped his hat to his opponents and expressed pride in his own lineup, saying, "Atlanta was the better club, but our guys really played hard. This experience is something we hope to build off of."

# OPENING DAY FIESTA!

When people think of baseball, they think of hot dogs, Cracker Jacks, and . . . burritos? Although baseball has long been known as America's national pastime, there have been many attempts during Bud Selig's tenure as baseball commissioner to create greater international interest in the game. In 1996, the New York Mets and San Diego Padres started a tradition that at least one major-league game of the season would be played on foreign soil. For their 1999 season opener, the Rockies traveled across the border for the first time in franchise history to take on the Padres in Monterrey, Mexico. It was a special day for the Rockies' popular third baseman, Vinny Castilla, who was highly regarded in Mexico because he was one of only a handful of Mexican-born players to have had a successful career in the majors. On this night, in front of family, friends, and a multitude of admirers, Castilla raised his game another notch to go four-for-five with a double to help the Rockies crush the defending NL champion Padres 8–2. Left fielder Dante Bichette, who also had a spectacular night, gave his teammate credit for the win, saying, it "was all because Vinny's hitting behind me. It's Vinnny's day."

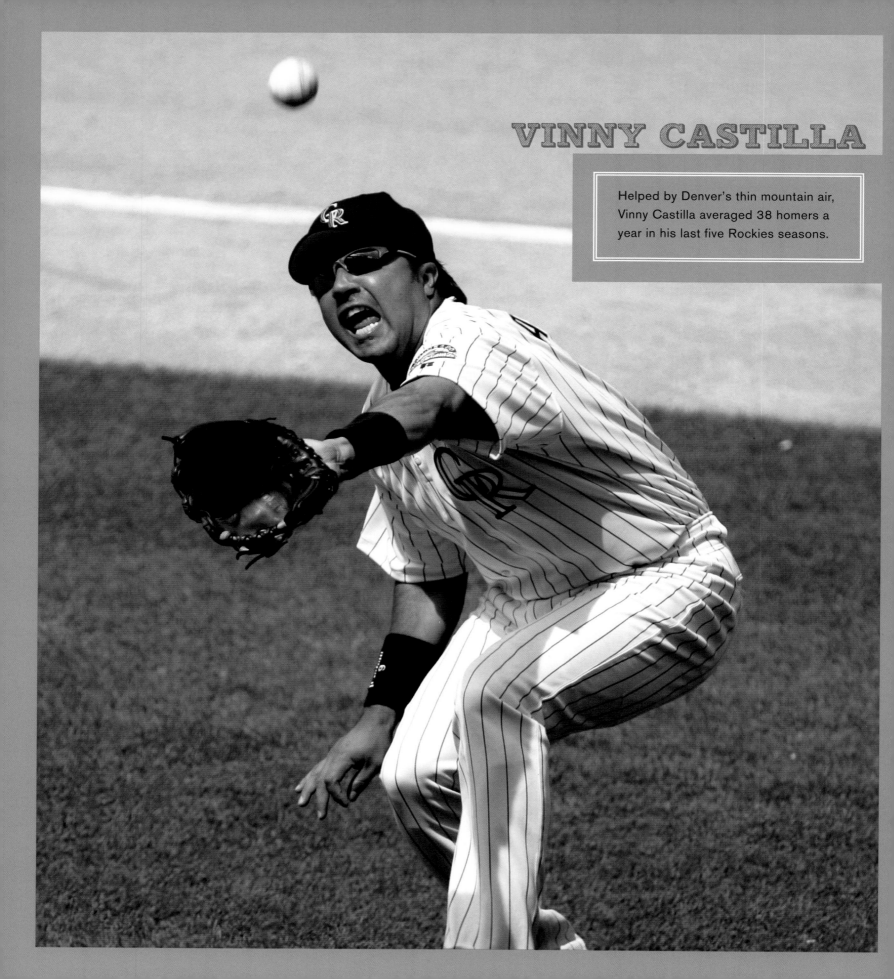

# VINNY CASTILLA

Helped by Denver's thin mountain air, Vinny Castilla averaged 38 homers a year in his last five Rockies seasons.

## SECOND BASEMAN · ERIC YOUNG

While the big bats of the "Blake Street Bombers" provided punch to the Rockies' lineup in the mid-1990s, Eric Young provided consistent hitting and speed on the base paths. A contact hitter who could send the ball into gaps for extra bases or drop down a perfect bunt to move a base runner into scoring position, Young's base-running ability was his calling card throughout his major-league career. In 1996, he tied a major-league record by stealing six bases in one game against the Los Angeles Dodgers, cementing his legacy as one of the elite speedsters of the '90s.

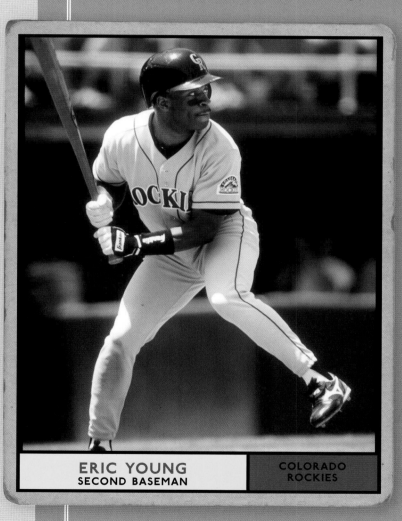

ERIC YOUNG
SECOND BASEMAN

COLORADO
ROCKIES

### STATS

**Rockies seasons: 1993–97**

**Height: 5-9**

**Weight: 185**

- **465 career stolen bases**

- **.283 career BA**

- **1,731 career hits**

- **1996 All-Star**

# JOE GIRARDI

**JOE GIRARDI** — Girardi was an unspectacular but always reliable backstop for five different pro teams. Known for his intelligent approach to the game, he made a smooth transition to big-league managing after hanging up his cleats in 2003.

# THE HUNT FOR OCTOBER

T he next few years featured seasons of frustration for the Rockies organization. After getting a taste of the postseason in 1995, the club and its fans were eager to take the next step and go deep into the 1996 playoffs, and it seemed as if Colorado had the team to do it. The Rockies added another powerful bat to the lineup by signing outfielder Ellis Burks, but they held steady at 83–79 in 1996 and 1997, mired in third place. They remained a formidable offensive force, though, despite their mediocre divisional standings; in 1996, Colorado became the first team in major-league history to post 200 home runs and 200 stolen bases in the same season, and Andres Galarraga set a club record for RBI in a season with 150.

The following few years saw many franchise firsts. In 1997, Larry Walker became the club's first Gold Glove winner (as the league's top defensive right fielder) and slugged his way to the NL's Most Valuable Player (MVP) award. On June 10, 1998, Bichette became the first Rockies player to bat for the cycle, hitting a single, double, triple, and home run all in the same game. Then, in a game against the Chicago Cubs on May 5, 1999, the Rockies scored in every inning of a nine-inning game, becoming just the third team in history

Ellis Burks had the best season of his career in 1996, finishing with 40 homers, 128 RBI, and a .344 average.

ELLIS BURKS

# SWINGING FOR THE STARS

Even though the Rockies have not fared particularly well in the baseball standings over the years, the unwavering devotion of their fans caught the attention of Major League Baseball enough that officials granted Colorado the honor of hosting the 1998 All-Star Game at Denver's Coors Field. The notion of bringing some of the game's greatest sluggers, such as Barry Bonds, Mark McGwire, and Jim Thome, together in the thin air of Colorado intrigued fans and players alike. Everyone expected a high-scoring game dominated by offense. But All-Star pitchers are invited to the game for a reason as well, and they held a tight leash on the powerful bats until San

Diego Padres right fielder Tony Gwynn ripped a two-run single in the third inning, opening the floodgates. Three players hit home runs, including a mammoth third-deck homer by San Francisco Giants left fielder Barry Bonds, in what would be the highest-scoring All-Star Game in major-league history. In the end, the American League (AL) beat the NL 13–8. Baseball fans around the country who watched the 1998 All-Star Game got a taste of typical Colorado baseball as they witnessed towering home runs and saw the two teams combine for an All-Star Game record of 31 hits.

## THIRD BASEMAN · VINNY CASTILLA

Few Rockies players captured the hearts and imaginations of Colorado fans the way Vinny Castilla did in the team's early years. Castilla's glove work at the "hot corner" was impressive, and from 1995 through 1999, his bat was smoking hot; he averaged 38 home runs and 112 RBI per season and was a pivotal part of Colorado's 1995 playoff run. "It didn't matter if he was speeding past motorists on Santa Fe Boulevard with his bright yellow Lamborghini or hitting a long home run," Rockies manager Clint Hurdle said in 2006. "Vinny Castilla was one of the faces of the Colorado Rockies franchise."

VINNY CASTILLA
THIRD BASEMAN

COLORADO ROCKIES

### STATS

**Rockies seasons: 1993–99, 2004, 2006**

**Height: 6-1**

**Weight: 185**

- **2-time All-Star**

- **.276 career BA**

- **320 career HR**

- **.966 career fielding percentage**

## SHORTSTOP · JUAN URIBE

Uribe made a splash with the Rockies in 2001, when he played in 72 games with the big-league club. Even though he suited up for less than half of the games that season, his 11 triples were second-most in the NL. He followed up his rookie campaign by playing a full season in the big leagues and leading all shortstops with 261 putouts. To continue developing his baseball skills, Uribe played winter ball each year in his native Dominican Republic. Uribe was traded to the Chicago White Sox after the 2003 season and was a vital part of their World Series championship team in 2005.

**JUAN URIBE**
**SHORTSTOP**

COLORADO
ROCKIES

### STATS

**Rockies seasons: 2001–03**

**Height: 5-11**

**Weight: 173**

- **.975 career fielding percentage**

- **.258 career BA**

- **141 career doubles**

- **32 career triples**

to accomplish the feat. Yet even as the accomplishments piled up, the team remained far from playoff contention.

After Colorado was well on its way to a fourth-place finish in 1998, Rockies management decided to part ways with the only manager the franchise had ever known, Don Baylor. Looking for a new spark, Colorado hired Jim Leyland, who had led the Florida Marlins to victory in the 1997 World Series.

Dreams for the future were put on hold, however, when tragedy struck close to home on April 20, 1999. Shootings at Columbine High School in nearby Littleton, Colorado, claimed the lives of 15 people, shaking the American public. Some members of the Rockies organization had children who attended Columbine, and the mood turned somber for the team. On April 21, Rockies vice chairman Charlie Monfort spoke of the horrific events, saying, "We are deeply saddened by the events in Littleton yesterday, and now is not the time to play baseball." Out of respect for the families affected by the shootings and for the people of Littleton, the Rockies postponed two games and, as a sign of remembrance, added a Columbine High School patch to the right sleeves of their uniforms for the rest of the season.

As the new millennium loomed, the Rockies were still searching for answers as to how they could consistently win in the high-altitude Rocky Moun-

## LEFT FIELDER · DANTE BICHETTE

One of the original Rockies, Dante Bichette's sweet swing was made for the hitter's paradise of Coors Field. A key power threat from 1993 through 1999, Bichette was not only the first player to hit a home run in a Rockies uniform, but he was also the first Rockies player to hit one out of Coors Field. A crucial cog in Colorado's 1995 playoff team, Bichette, who came close to having a Triple Crown season by hitting .340 with 40 home runs and 128 RBI, led the NL in six different hitting categories that year. He also posted a 23-game hitting streak that still stands as a Rockies record.

**DANTE BICHETTE**
LEFT FIELDER

COLORADO
ROCKIES

### STATS

**Rockies seasons: 1993–99**

**Height: 6-3**

**Weight: 225**

- **4-time All-Star**

- **1995 NL leader in HR (40)**

- **274 career HR**

- **.299 career BA**

tains. They needed to find a pitcher who was able to induce a lot of ground balls and prevent batters from slamming home runs. The Rockies found him in Pedro Astacio, who tied the team record for wins with 17 in 1999. But after ending that season in fifth place, the club released Leyland and handed the reins to new manager Buddy Bell. Colorado brass then traded longtime fan favorites Vinny Castilla and Dante Bichette for four players who would remain in Colorado for only one season. Bell had his work cut out for him.

**TODD HELTON** – An All-Star every year from 2000 to 2004, the first baseman was known for his surprisingly powerful swing and sharp eye at the plate. In 2000 and 2001, he became the first player ever to get 100 extra-base hits in back-to-back seasons.

Pedro Astacio won a career-high 17 games in 1999
despite giving up a league-worst 38 home runs.

# THE NEW MILLENNIUM

The Rockies opened the 2000 season with more than just a new manager and new optimism. New purple jerseys were added as well as an alternate home uniform, making the Rockies stand out in the major leagues as the only team to have purple as its dominant color. However, the biggest change for the Rockies was on the field, where only six players from the 1999 opening day roster remained.

The new Rockies were built less for slugging long balls and more for hitting for average, playing solid defense, and pitching. Two sure-gloved players who hit for high average, third baseman Jeff Cirillo and left fielder Jeffrey Hammonds, stepped in to replace Castilla and Bichette.

On August 22, 2000, the Rockies played what may have been the strangest game in team history as they took on the Atlanta Braves at Coors Field. In a close battle that went into extra innings, the Rockies used 10 different pitchers in the first 11 innings. As they entered the 12th inning, the Rockies faced a dilemma: they were out of fresh pitchers. New Rockies catcher Brent Mayne took the mound and pitched a scoreless inning, and backup catcher Adam Melhuse drove in the winning run in the bottom of the inning to give

### CENTER FIELDER · JUAN PIERRE

Sometimes it pays to trust a thief. Two-thirds of the way through the 2000 season, the Rockies introduced Juan Pierre to the major leagues, and no base—in any park—has been safe ever since. Although the speedy center fielder stole only seven bases that first year, he went on to lead the NL with 46 thefts in 2001. On a team known for its ability to slug the ball into the stands, Pierre was a contact hitter who used his speed to not only get on base but to take extra bases as well. Pierre's fleet feet made him a wide-ranging center fielder and a perennial fan favorite.

JUAN PIERRE
CENTER FIELDER

COLORADO
ROCKIES

### STATS

**Rockies seasons: 2000–02**

**Height: 6-0**

**Weight: 180**

- **.991 career fielding average**

- **325 career stolen bases**

- **.303 career BA**

- **2-time NL leader in stolen bases**

the Rockies a narrow 7–6 victory. Mayne got the decision, becoming the first major-league position player to earn a pitching victory since outfielder Rocky Colavito won a game for the New York Yankees in 1968.

Unfortunately, the Rockies came up short of the playoffs again that season, finishing with an 82–80 mark and in fourth place in the NL West. In December, the team sought to solidify a shaky pitching staff by signing two of the biggest names on the free-agent market, the New York Yankees' Denny Neagle and New York Mets' Mike Hampton, for a combined $17.7 million for the 2001 season. When asked about pitching in the thin air of Colorado, Neagle said, "I really believe half the thing about pitching in [Denver] is that a lot of pitchers psyche themselves out before they get here, and I admit I used to be one of those guys."

The move seemed to pay off as Hampton became the first Rockies pitcher to be named to an All-Star team in 2001. Near the end of July, the Rockies made a trade with the Houston Astros, giving up franchise wins leader Pedro Astacio for Colorado native Scott Elarton. Unfortunately, after pitching just 23 innings for the Rockies in 2001, a shoulder injury forced Elarton to miss the entire 2002 season. The thin mountain air seemed to take effect as well, as both Hampton and Neagle saw their earned run averages (ERAs) rise dramatically. Hampton, who had consistently kept his ERA below 4.00 on other teams, watched the number skyrocket to 5.41 in his first season and 6.15 in his second with the Rockies. The pair's combined 23–21 record in 2001 was below expectations, and Colorado sank to last place in its division.

## THE MILE-HIGH EQUALIZER

Denver's Coors Field is the ultimate hitter's park. Although the field dimensions are fairly spacious, the thin air at nearly a mile above sea level provides little resistance to a baseball in flight, which causes a dual problem for pitchers: breaking balls such as curveballs and sliders need air resistance to provide movement; without it, the pitch doesn't break, making the ball easier to hit. And the ball, once it is hit, can travel faster and farther without the normal air resistance. In the spring of 2002, the Rockies developed a plan to even out the effects of the thin air by installing a walk-in humidor at Coors Field. The humidor, in which the baseballs are stored, is intended to keep the balls in their original condition. The atmosphere of Coors Field typically dries the balls out and makes them light and slick, which compounds the effects of the thin air. Although some have questioned the science behind the move, the results appear to have proven it legitimate. Since the humidor was added, the average number of runs scored per game at Coors Field (15) has dropped closer to the major-league average of 9.

ROCKIES

## RIGHT FIELDER · LARRY WALKER

When the Rockies felt that they were close to contending for a pennant before the 1995 season, they made a big move by signing the most prolific Canadian-born position player in the history of the game: Larry Walker. The right fielder rewarded them by slugging 36 home runs, driving in 101 runs, and batting .306 during his first season in Colorado. Before he was traded away in 2004, he held nearly every offensive club record. A potential Hall-of-Famer, Walker retired after helping lead the St. Louis Cardinals to the World Series in 2004 and the NL Championship Series in 2005.

### STATS

**Rockies seasons: 1995–2004**

**Height: 6-3**

**Weight: 215**

- **383 career HR**

- **5-time All-Star**

- **7-time Gold Glove winner**

- **1997 NL MVP**

**LARRY WALKER**
RIGHT FIELDER

COLORADO
ROCKIES

## THE WORLD MEETS THE ROCKIES

The spring of 2006 saw the beginning of the World Baseball Classic (WBC), a bracket-style playoff series among 16 baseball teams from all around the world. This event, set to occur every four years, gives major- and minor-league players the opportunity to represent their native countries on the field and serves to create greater international exposure for the game of baseball. Commissioner Bud Selig was pleased with the success of the new venture, saying, "I admit I went in believing it would be good, but this has really, really been good." For major-league teams, though, it can mean opening up spring training without all of their stars. Sixteen players from the Rockies system were placed on provisional rosters for the World Classic on teams from countries such as the U.S., Canada, and Korea. When the final rosters had been set, eight members of the Rockies organization were selected to participate in the WBC, representing five different countries. Having so many players participate illustrated the depth of Rockies scouting in the international market. Catcher Miguel Ojeda launched a home run in one game for his native Mexico, and pitcher Byung-Hyun Kim helped Korea make it to the semifinals by picking up a victory and seven strikeouts in four appearances.

ROCKIES

**DARREN OLIVER** – Colorado's mountain air seemed to rejuvenate Oliver's struggling career. In 2003, his first and only season with the Rockies, he won 13 games—his highest total in six years. That season, he also slugged his only big-league home run.

# BUILDING FOR THE FUTURE

T he emergence of pitcher Jason Jennings, who went 16–8 and won the NL Rookie of the Year award in 2002, gave the Rockies reason to believe that better times were ahead. Hoping to mimic the success of Jennings, Rockies management continued to bring in pitchers with good sinking pitches who could get opposing batters to keep the ball on the ground, taking the home run out of play. Unfortunately, few could match Jennings' consistency. The closest anyone came to Jennings' mark in 2002 was Dennis Stark, who won 11 games. Jennings became the one reliable fixture in a rotation that saw constant change throughout the 2002 season.

In yet another attempt to shake the team from its losing ways, Rockies management fired Buddy Bell as manager in 2002 and promoted hitting coach Clint Hurdle, a favorite among the players. "You hate to call your manager a big goof-ball, but he is," said Larry Walker. "He's full of excitement, he's fun, and he jokes around. He's brought a new spirit to the clubhouse and the bench."

From 2002 through 2004, Colorado remained stuck in fourth place in the NL West. During that time, only Jennings, Darren Oliver, and closer Shawn Chacon remained consistent cogs in the club's pitching staff. After Walker was

PRESTON WILSON

## MANAGER · DON BAYLOR

Who better to take on the painful task of managing an expansion franchise than a former major-leaguer who led the AL in getting hit by pitches in eight different seasons? Don Baylor's first years as manager of the Rockies had their rough moments and setbacks, but Baylor was able to take those early hits and then lead the team to its finest seasons during his six years as skipper. In 1995, he led Colorado to the playoffs for the first and only time in franchise history and was named NL Manager of the Year. After the Rockies let Baylor go, he went on to manage the Chicago Cubs from 2000 to 2002.

### STATS

**Rockies seasons as manager: 1993–98**

**Height: 6-1**

**Weight: 195**

**Managerial Record: 627–689**

**Playoff Appearances: 1995 Wild Card**

**DON BAYLOR**
**MANAGER**

COLORADO
ROCKIES

GARRETT ATKINS

traded to the St. Louis Cardinals in August 2004, first baseman Todd Helton represented the only link to the days of the Blake Street Bombers. But Colorado fans were soon cheering for a new procession of long-ball bombers. First it was center fielder Preston Wilson—who slugged 36 home runs and contributed 141 RBI in 2003, his first year with the team—and then it was journeyman outfielder Jeromy Burnitz, who signed with Colorado before the 2004 season. Both players could clear the fences and drive in runs, but both also posted high strikeout numbers.

The Rockies continued trying to put a winning team on the field the next two seasons, but their approach changed as the club turned to its minor-league system to produce young talent. Up-and-coming prospects such as left fielder Matt Holliday and third baseman Garrett Atkins showed promise in 2005 and then became slugging stars in 2006. The Rockies made another key move by trading Jennings away in 2006 to obtain potential star pitcher Jason Hirsh. This commitment to youth resulted in two more losing campaigns in 2005 and 2006, but the team headed into its 15th season in 2007 believing it was ready to challenge for its first NL West title.

The Colorado faithful who have poured into the stands at Coors Field for more than a decade to cheer on the home team may finally have reason for hope. With veteran leader Todd Helton shepherding a promising young line-up, Rockies fans are optimistic that their mile-high team will soon soar back to the playoffs and fight their way to baseball's ultimate stage, the World Series.

ROCKIES

# INDEX